Caught on the Hop

A play

David Foxton

Samuel French—London
New York-Toronto-Hollywood

Please see page iv for further copyright information

CHARACTERS

Clothilde, a maid
Sophie Fontaineau, the lady of the house
Etienne Fontaineau, her husband
A Porter
"Esmeralda"

The action of the play takes place in a room or
hallway of a Paris apartment.

Time–1890-1900

Other plays by David Foxton,
published by Samuel French Ltd

Card Play
The Crowns, The King and the Long Lost Smile
Perkin and the Pastrycook
Rabbit

CAUGHT ON THE HOP

A room or hallway in the Paris apartment of Monsieur and Madame Fontaineau. The room has three doors: one leads to Madame Fontaineau's bedroom and to that of Clothilde, the maid, another to Monsieur Fontaineau's bedroom and the third to the stairs that lead to the street. Essential items of furniture are chairs, or chairs and a chaise longue, a screen and a table with a bottle of brandy and glasses on it

Before the CURTAIN *rises a doorbell rings, then again and yet again, somewhat frantically; then the ringing becomes really urgent. During this, the* CURTAIN *rises*

The stage is in darkness. Clothilde enters from her bedroom in her night attire, with her hair in rags and carrying a light. She stumbles sleepily across towards the street door, blundering into items of furniture on her way

Clothilde All right! All right! I'm coming as quickly as I can. Don't be so impatient. It's the middle of the night, for heaven's sake. I hear you! Merde! (*To the audience*) Why can't they be in bed like any normal human being? Perhaps it's the police. (*To the door*) All right, I'm on my way!

She exits through the street door

(*Off*) Coming! I'm on my way!

Sophie (*off*) It's all right, I've found a key. Don't worry, Clothilde.

Sophie, Madame Fontaineau, enters from the street, wearing an outdoor coat and a veiled hat and carrying a handbag. She is followed by Clothilde

Clothilde (*counting*) Thirty-three, thirty-four, thirty-five, thirty-six ...

Sophie Where on earth were you, Clothilde? I've been ringing and ringing. I thought I'd have woken the whole house.

Clothilde (*taking Sophie's coat and hat*) I was in bed, madame.

Sophie Bed! Bed! And sleeping no doubt too. Fast asleep if I know you. (*To the audience*) Really, servants these days are so selfish.

Clothilde It is half-past two, madame ——

Sophie (*to the audience*) — I can remember when servants couldn't even tell the time — now they thrust it at you ——

Clothilde — a.m. ...

Sophie You see what I mean. (*To Clothilde*) And you don't need to tell me what time it is. I know full well the time; every part of my body is aching with the time. I've been travelling for hours and hours. Have you any conception of the distances I've travelled today, Clothilde?

Clothilde You've been to visit your great aunt in the country, madame.

Sophie I know where I've been, Clothilde. It is how long it took that matters.

Clothilde About six hours.

Sophie It took six hours! Six long and uncomfortable hours! Six there and six back. That's — a long time. And every moment was an agony. I felt every bump on the way. I'm just longing to fall into bed.

Clothilde I know how you feel, madame.

Sophie How can you possibly? What a thing to say! I travel all the way to Beauvais to be with her for the weekend. (*To the audience*) My only remaining great aunt. I have so very few relatives. (*To Clothilde*) So I go there to comfort her — six hours — to minister to the sick, to mop her fevered brow and administer soothing broths and the like — and what do I find?

Clothilde shrugs, looking ignorant

I'll tell you what I find. I find that Great Aunt Marie-Louise has been inconsiderate enough to die without my being there — before I arrived. (*To the audience*) Such lack of control.

Clothilde Oh, dear, I am sorry, madame.

Sophie Ten minutes before I got there, the maid said.

Clothilde No wonder you're upset.

Sophie Another servant adamant about the time — ten minutes, she said she was certain.

Clothilde Had she been ill long?

Sophie I mean you would think she could have hung on for a measly ten minutes.

Clothilde How old was she?

Sophie All the rest of my family had constitutions like ... like ... what are those large animals, Clothilde?

Clothilde Where, madame?

Sophie It doesn't matter where — what are they?

Clothilde I really couldn't say, madame, we had the rat-catcher round barely two weeks ago. He found nothing.

Sophie From Africa.

Clothilde Was he? I never realized.

Sophie No, the animals. Big and serviceable — last forever.

Clothilde No, I don't think so — not here anyway. I'd have noticed.

Sophie Rhinoceroses, that's them, rhinoceroses.

Clothilde I think he'd have mentioned them, them rhino — what you said's. He'd got traps for almost anything.

Sophie She could have let me know if she didn't think she'd last. I could have been spared the journey — all that luggage ...

A Porter enters from the street, laden with luggage. He collapses exhaustedly

(*To the Porter*) Leave them there, will you? Good gracious me, my man, you look on your last legs. You really shouldn't have offered to carry my bags up if you weren't capable. Clothilde, get the man a chair. I really can't stomach the thought of two corpses in one day.

Clothilde fetches a chair and helps the Porter on to it

Clothilde (*to the audience*) What surprises me is that she should kill off her aunt in the country so easily. I mean she was such a convenient excuse for a weekend away.

Sophie (*searching in her handbag*) And here's a little something for your immense trouble — nothing! Absolutely nothing! I gave my last sous to the crossing sweeper. Don't worry, just recover yourself. I'll get some money from my husband. (*She calls off*) Etienne! Etienne!

Sophie exits to her husband's room

Clothilde (*to the audience*) You see I never believed the great aunt existed, not before; now she's dead I can believe in her better. (*To the Porter*) You look awful!

The Porter indicates the luggage

I know — she always takes too many things away with her.

The Porter mimes the stairs and the distance

I know! All those steps! How many do you think there are? I'll tell you. Thirty-four, well, thirty-six if you count the two up to the front door. Did you?

The Porter still can't speak

Not many people do. I do though. Every blessed time. Haven't I seen you somewhere before?

He shakes his head

You could do with a drink, you know.

He nods his head. Clothilde moves to the table to pour a glass of brandy

(*To the audience*) It's my suspicious nature, you know. A great aunt in the country, weekends away; most useful — I wouldn't put it past her ... (*To the Porter*) It's a young man's job, carrying luggage. You've quite worn yourself out. You ought to get yourself a better job.

Sophie enters

Sophie Oh Clothilde! Clothilde! Oh Clothilde! (*She takes the glass of brandy from Clothilde and drinks it*)
Clothilde Oh madame! Madame! Oh madame! What is it?
Sophie What is it?
Clothilde Brandy! I was just giving him a nip — for his condition.
Sophie Clothilde! My husband!

Clothilde No, the porter; he's worn out ...

Sophie My husband — Etienne!

Clothilde That's right, *that's* your husband.

Sophie He's — he's — oh, Clothilde, he's — not in his room.

Clothilde That's right, madame. (*She turns and pours another brandy*)

Sophie You mean you know?

Clothilde Oh yes, madame. (*To the Porter, handing him a glass of brandy*) Now come along and drink this; you'll feel all the better for it.

Sophie The swine! The minute I leave town. The very moment my back is turned, he's away! Off! God only knows where — and with whom. Men! I should have known! Making the most of his freedom! The deceiver! Typical! I'll bet he just couldn't wait for the front door to close behind me.

Clothilde (*to the Porter*) It warms you right through, doesn't it? Do you feel better?

The Porter nods

Would you like another?

The Porter nods

Sophie "Another!" "Another!" How can you say such things, Clothilde?

Clothilde (*to the audience, pouring another brandy*) He's usually been home when she's come back from one of her weekends visiting ... the sick.

Sophie That's where he is! That must be the answer! (*To the Porter*) Oh, sir! Oh, sir! You must forgive this outburst, you really must! I realize it must be an embarrassing situation for you. I can but try to hold back the torrent of my emotions. But when your husband deceives you in such an underhand and yet wholly obvious way, what can a poor rejected woman do?

Clothilde (*to the audience*) It's the first time she's missed him.

Porter Madame, I ——

Sophie No, don't say anything! Don't tell me. You're a man, aren't you? How can you possibly understand?

Clothilde (*taking the glass of brandy to the Porter*) Here you are.

Sophie Thank you, thank you, Clothilde. (*She takes the glass of brandy from Clothilde*) You understand — you know — you share — you feel like I do — you too are aware of what has happened ——

Clothilde Yes, madame ——

Sophie Oh Clothilde!

Clothilde He's gone to his Literary Society meeting.

Sophie Quite! You're so right! I couldn't have put it better myself — he's gone where?

Clothilde The Literary Society meeting.

Sophie What?

Clothilde Every second Friday.

Sophie Is it?

Clothilde You go to see your great aunt and monsieur goes to the Literary Society.

Sophie How — convenient.

Clothilde Yes, it has been.

Sophie The Literary Society.

Clothilde Regular as clockwork. A real supporter of literature is Monsieur Fontaineau.

Sophie I never remember seeing him read anything but the newspaper.

Clothilde I think he might even be an officer of the Society.

Sophie Really?

Porter I'm feeling better now, madame. I don't need another brandy. I'll be getting back to ——

Sophie No! No! I won't think of it! Not until I've given you a little something for your pains. My husband — he's an officer in the Literary Society, you know — will be home shortly, I'm sure. Clothilde, a brandy for monsieur.

Porter You're too kind.

Sophie Of course, the second Friday, I'm sure he must have mentioned it. What a fool I am, my head always full of my concern for Great Aunt Marie-Louise; such a good woman. The grief, it's just hitting me; she was so good, so very good. (*She snivels*) I shall miss her so very much. (*She snivels some more*)

Porter (*proffering a handkerchief*) Borrow my handkerchief, madame.

Sophie (*taking the handkerchief*) Thank you! Thank you! I shall ensure that my husband doubles his pourboire.

Porter No! No! It's nothing!

Sophie To me, a distraught woman, it is everything, a morceau of comfort in my time of abject distress. Did he say what time he'd be back, Clothilde?

Clothilde Alas, no, madame. He just said that I needn't wait up; he'd let himself in, he said.

Sophie Such a thoughtful and considerate man, my husband.

Porter I'm sure he is, madame.

Sophie (*to the Porter*) Haven't I seen you somewhere before?

Porter Somewhere before?

Clothilde He brought your luggage up.

Sophie Of course he did. What a kind man, what a very kind man. Clothilde, a brandy for Monsieur——? Monsieur——?

Clothilde takes the Porter's glass and pours him another brandy

Porter Er — er — Monsieur — Fragonard ...

Sophie Fragonard. What a pleasant name — Fragonard.

Porter My parents gave me it.

Sophie Parents can be so useful that way.

Clothilde (*handing the glass to the Porter*) Your brandy, Monsieur Fragonard.

Porter Thank you.

Sophie (*suddenly*) But he can't find me like this, with a strange man at — er ——

Clothilde Two forty-five a.m.

Sophie What would Etienne say?

Porter I'll go!

Sophie No, you must stay; I owe you so much.

Porter What then?

Sophie Sit down.

Sophie pushes the Porter down; he spills brandy on his trousers

Oh, monsieur, forgive me ——

Porter No it's all right. It's nothing, nothing, I do assure you.

Sophie Clothilde, dry this kind man's trousers at once. I cannot apologize enough, monsieur. I must prepare myself for bed. Etienne would never forgive me for waiting up for him; he'd think that I didn't trust him, that I was a scheming and suspicious wife. Take your trousers off, Monsieur Fragonard.

Porter Eh?

Clothilde (*to the Porter*) She means you. Come on, take them off; I'll dry and iron them in no time at all!

Porter But no, really, I insist ...

Sophie Come now, monsieur, surely you can't imagine that my maid and I are suggesting anything improper?

Porter Of course not.

Sophie Then take your trousers off man, while I get ready for bed!

Sophie exits to her bedroom

Porter What?

Clothilde Come on! Give me your trousers. It's time I was in bed too!

Porter What? (*He removes his trousers*)

Clothilde (*taking the trousers from the Porter*) Better give me
   your jacket also. It looks as though a good press wouldn't do it
   any harm!

Porter No, thank you. It's all right, really.

Clothilde (*removing the Porter's jacket*) Looks as though you
   sleep in it. I won't be more than a few minutes, I do assure you.

*Clothilde exits in the direction of her bedroom with the Porter's
jacket and trousers*

Porter Oh dear! Oh dear! What a situation!

Sophie (*off*) Clothilde, you will look after Monsieur Fragonard,
   won't you?

Clothilde (*off*) Leave it to me, madame.

Porter Oh dear, oh dear ... (*He wanders about aimlessly, out of
   his depth: he might sit momentarily*)

Sophie (*off*) My husband won't be long, monsieur, you can
   depend on that.

Porter Oh dear! Oh dear!

*The bell begins to ring and continues to do so under the following
dialogue*

   Oh dear! Oh dearie dear! (*He hides behind the screen*)

Sophie (*off*) Front door, Clothilde!

Clothilde enters and heads for the street door

Clothilde I hear it! I hear it!

Sophie (*off*) Someone at the front door, Clothilde!

Clothilde I heard you! I heard you! (*She looks around the room*)
   Monsieur Fragonard?

The Porter peers out

Won't be a moment — so sorry!

Sophie enters from her bedroom in night attire

Sophie Clothilde! Can you not hear the bell?
Clothilde I'm on my way! How many times?
Sophie It could be Monsieur Fontaineau, my Etienne.
Clothilde No, madame. He has his own key; he leaves it under the doormat. Coming!

Clothilde exits to the street

Sophie Under the doormat! But that's the key I used to let myself in — Where on earth did I put it? (*She looks around the room, then behind the screen. She screams*) Help! It's a man! It's a man!
Porter No it isn't, it's me, Madame Fontaineau. You remember me?
Sophie Monsieur Delacroix?
Porter That's close enough.
Sophie Stay where you are; my husband may not understand ...
Porter I understand.
Sophie Don't come out until I introduce you.
Porter Right!
Sophie I'll wait in my bedroom.

Sophie exits to her bedroom

Etienne Fontaineau enters from the street dressed as the Hunchback of Notre Dame. He falls over the cases

Clothilde enters from the street

Clothilde Thirty-three, thirty-four, thirty-five, thirty-six.

Clothilde helps Etienne to his feet

Etienne And who left these here? And where's my key? And why
    didn't you answer the door quicker? I've been ringing the bell
    for almost ten minutes, I'm sure. Where were you, Clothilde?

Clothilde On my way. I didn't know it was you, monsieur. It is
    you, isn't it, monsieur?

Etienne Of course it's me, Clothilde.

Clothilde But monsieur, the — outfit, the — costume.

Etienne Never mind that. It's part of your duties to answer the
    door, isn't it?

Clothilde What are you supposed to be?

Etienne Don't worry about that ... And why aren't you in bed
    asleep?

Clothilde I had to get up to answer the door.

Etienne That was me.

Clothilde But monsieur has his own key ——

Etienne — which he left safe and secure under the doormat as
    usual.

Clothilde So I knew you could let yourself in; you wouldn't need
    to ring the bell.

Etienne Except that the key isn't there any more. Didn't such a
    possibility ever cross the desert of your mind?

Clothilde Not until now, monsieur.

Etienne Ideas are as foreign to your brain, Clothilde, as dolphins
    are to the Sahara.

Clothilde If you say so, sir!

Sophie (*off*) Is that you, Etienne — my darling?

Etienne Who's that — in there, Clothilde?

Clothilde I've no idea, sir — no idea at all.

Clothilde exits to her bedroom

Etienne Clothilde! Clothilde! Come back here! Oh Lord, now I've upset her. Why can't anything go right for me? My wife away for the weekend, everything planned: the costume ball at the *Moulin Rouge*, a pretty little "Esmeralda" all lined up, and the door key goes missing and I have to wake the maid ——

Sophie (*off*) Etienne! Etienne, is that you?

Etienne Yes dear, it's me. Now where the devil can it have got to? I told my little Esmeralda I'd leave it under the mat, then she could creep in — Sophie! Oh, my God, Sophie! (*A little louder*) Sophie! Is that you?

Sophie (*off*) Come to bed, my little sweet pea.

Etienne (*to the audience*) What happened to the great aunt?

Sophie (*off*) Come on, my own Etienne. It's a surprise for you.

Etienne (*to the audience*) She never spoke a truer word. Oh, my goodness gracious, what when my Esmeralda arrives? What time is it?

The Porter holds out his watch from behind the screen

Just after three — thank you — and I told her to be here by quarter past.

Sophie (*off*) Etienne, what's keeping you?

Etienne Coming, my little one, I'm coming — ho hum. (*He fakes a yawn*) Just having a night cap. (*He moves to the drinks table and rattles the bottles and glasses. To the audience*) What can I do? She'll suspect something if I wait much longer. I'll go and placate her and then sneak away; but wait, she can't see me like this, she'll know I've been celebrating ... and what a night, what a ball, everyone dressed as characters from French Literature — a glittering occasion ...

Sophie (*off*) Etienne, what are you up to?

Etienne Nothing, my love! Coming my love! She'll drop off to sleep in no time. What can I put on? (*He sees Sophie's coat*) Ah, just the job, just the thing. (*He puts his hand in the coat pocket*)

But what's this — in the pocket? (*He produces a key from the pocket*) A key, a door key, a house door key, *my* house door key.

Clothilde enters with the Porter's trousers and jacket

Clothilde Here we are. I said it wouldn't take long, Monsieur Fragonard.

Etienne Quasimodo! Have you no literary knowledge? (*He sees the trousers and jacket*) Clothilde, ah ha, you little wonder, you life-saver, my reputation is saved ... (*He takes the clothes from her*)

Clothilde But sir——

Etienne Listen, take this key and go and put it under the front-door mat, quickly, quickly!

Clothilde But you're already in, sir.

Etienne Do it! Do it! Do it! (*To the audience*) I don't want anyone ringing the doorbell.

Clothilde (*to the audience*) I've almost forgotten what it's like being in bed.

Clothilde negotiates the pile of luggage and exits to the street

Etienne Now, I don't need the coat, or the hat. (*He tosses the coat and hat over the screen*) I'll just put my clothes on. Oh, what a joy it is to have such a thoughtful maid. (*He takes his tunic off and throws it over the screen, leaving his hump in place; then he puts the trousers and jacket on*) Heavens, I didn't realize I was so fat. (*The actor can say "thin" if he happens not to be fat*) I must have put on (*Or "lost"*) a lot of weight recently. What a terrible fit! And the style — I really must change my tailor.

Sophie enters from her bedroom

Sophie Etienne, I can't wait for you any longer, my love, my own.

Etienne Sophie, my darling Sophie, what a surprise!

Sophie Etienne. (*She sees his hump and screams*) Aargh!

Etienne What is it?

Sophie There!

Etienne Where?

Sophie Behind you.

Etienne What? (*He turns round*)

Sophie Oh my God!

Etienne What is the matter, Sophie?

Sophie Your back!

Etienne Of course I am, and so are you. We are together once more. (*He makes to embrace her*)

Sophie Don't touch me! Don't you dare touch me! Why ever didn't you tell me about this?

Etienne So you've guessed.

Sophie Guessed? Guessed? One would have to be blind not to have realized.

Etienne It's only once a year.

Sophie Something to do with the moon is it? Like those werewolf things ——

Etienne It's just a bit of fun, that's all.

Sophie Fun? How can it be a bit of fun! It's ugly and degrading; why did you never mention it before?

Etienne You were visiting your great aunt.

Sophie It could have been taken away.

Etienne It *was* postponed one year.

Sophie Postponed?

Etienne They moved it.

Sophie Where did you have it then?

Etienne At the *Moulin de Galette*.

Clothilde enters from the street

Clothilde Thirty-bleeding-four, thirty-bleeding-five, thirty-bleed-ing-six!
Sophie Clothilde!
Clothilde (*pointing at Etienne*)What is it, madame?
Sophie Look! Look! Look!
Clothilde It's monsieur!
Sophie Look at him carefully, Clothilde.

Clothilde looks closely at Etienne

Etienne What on earth is the matter, Sophie?
Sophie What do you see?
Clothilde He's wearing someone else's suit.
Etienne Sssh!
Sophie Oh, thank heaven for that, I thought he was a hunchback.
Etienne (*realizing*) Hunchback? A hunchback? Ho ho! Ha ha!
   Goodness no, it's just the suit, it's the suit, that's all. Ha! Ha!
   A hunchback — what a thing to suggest!
Sophie What a mistake to make.
Etienne It's easily done, my love, don't worry. There! There!
Sophie Whose suit is it then, Etienne?
Etienne Whose suit?
Sophie Yes, whose suit?
Clothilde Monsieur Fragonard's.
Etienne Yes, that's it, it's Monsieur Fragonard's; he's a member
   of the Literary Society too. We — exchanged suits — for a —
   for a bet. He's a hunchback.
Sophie No he isn't.
Etienne How do you know?
Sophie Know what?
Etienne That Monsieur Fragonard isn't a hunchback.

Sophie You're up to something, Etienne Fontaineau, and I can prove it. I know that Monsieur Fragonard isn't a hunchback because — because ... (*She stops, realizing that she can't tell the truth, because this would expose her*)

Clothilde Because he's the rat-catcher.

Etienne Rat-catcher?

Clothilde Surely you knew, monsieur? (*She droops exhaustedly, nearly asleep*)

Sophie You and he being members of the same Literary Society and all that ——

Etienne Oh, rat-catcher. Yes, Fragonard the Rat-catcher. I thought you said "backscratcher". I knew he was a rat-catcher all the time, I've known it for years. In fact, I think we joined the Literary Society on the same day.

Sophie April the First?

Etienne Was it? Was it really? It doesn't seem so long ago. We were only talking about it this very night. "How's the rat—catching going, Fragonard?" I said. "Fine," he said, "fine!" "We've been members of the Society for a while now, haven't we?" I said. And he said ——

Sophie Are you telling the truth, Etienne?

Etienne What?

Sophie (*looking across at Clothilde*) Don't go to sleep, Clothilde, I want you to hear this!

Etienne What are you suggesting, Sophie?

Sophie I'm suggesting that a man who would hide from his wife the truth about his deformity would also hide other peccadilloes.

Etienne Peccadilloes, my love? What sort of peccadilloes? Clothilde, do I have any peccadilloes?

Clothilde Oh no, sir, we had the rat-catcher only two weeks ago.

Etienne Surely you don't suspect me of trifling, Sophie, my love?

Sophie But I do, Etienne, my darling, I do. In fact, I accuse you
now, you trifler. There's another woman in all this tomfoolery
somewhere and I mean to ferret her out.

Clothilde That's what the rat-catcher uses: ferrets.

Etienne No! It's enough! Sophie, I cannot hide the facts from
you any longer, I'll come clean and throw myself upon your
mercy ——

The Porter sneezes behind the screen

Bless you! How can I begin to ——

The Porter sneezes again

Bless you! It's like this ... (*He pauses*) Wait a moment, wait just
a moment. (*He picks up something to use as a weapon. To the
unseen Porter*) Come out, I know you're hiding there; come
out this very minute.

*The Porter, dressed in Sophie's hat and coat and Etienne's
discarded tunic, comes out*

What's — this?

There is a pause

Sophie Oh Great Aunt Marie-Louise, I'd forgotten all about you
behind there. Do come out. Etienne, this is my Great Aunt
Marie-Louise you've heard me talk so much about, and whom
I visit regularly. She's come back with me tonight because she
is far from well, far from well, isn't that true, Clothilde?

Clothilde She looks better now than when you first came home,
madame.

Sophie But she's far from good ...

The Porter sneezes again

Oh, Auntie, do take care.

Etienne Why was she hidden behind the screen?

Sophie Shyness is such a terrible thing, don't you agree? Many people don't realize what an affliction it is.

Clothilde There aren't many people who die of it, though.

Sophie Go back to sleep, Clothilde.

Etienne You're very welcome, Great Aunt-in-Law Marie-Louise. Sorry to hear you've not been well.

The Porter sneezes again

Bless you! I think Sophie should be putting you to bed.

Sophie What are you suggesting, Etienne?

Etienne It must be long past her bedtime, and with a cold like she has ——

The Porter sneezes

Bless you!

Porter It's not a cold: I'm allergic to fur.

Sophie (*quickly*) Another complication, Etienne; she's just a walking compendium of illnesses. I don't know how she manages to keep going!

Porter Thank you madame.

Etienne Wait a minute — there's something very familiar about you.

Sophie It must be a family likeness, you know how these things occur.

Etienne Just take your hat off a moment, Great Aunt-in-Law, if you'd be so kind.

Sophie Oh not tonight, Etienne, it's so late.

Etienne It won't take a minute. (*He moves to lift the veil on the Porter's hat*)

Esmeralda enters before the veil can be lifted. She is a little the worse for drink

Esmeralda Quazzi, here I am at last. (*She falls over the pile of cases*) Hell fire! Who left this bloody lot lying around? I've almost crippled myself. (*She laughs*) Where's the party? (*To Etienne*) You ought to have something done about those stairs. They'll finish you off one of these days, my little hunchback; you ain't got the stamina for 'em and that's a fact. Where's the booze?

Esmeralda moves towards the table. As she passes Sophie, she slaps her on the back. Sophie coughs through the next lines as a result of the slap

How you doin', me old love? Are you gonna make one in tonight an' all? (*She refers to Sophie's cough*) Dame aux Camellias, am I right? Where's your flowers? Don't remember you at the dancing. Sitting it out were you? Couldn't your chest stand it? (*She laughs*) Mind you it looks pretty pneumatic to me. (*She looks at the semi-dormant Clothilde*) Who's this? Don't tell me, let me guess — is it Zola? Tell me, Quazzi.

Sophie Who is this person?

Esmeralda Oh, very imperious, I like that; yes, good for you, give her a bit of real character. That's how I imagine Marguerite Gautier — very good. Would you like a drink?

Sophie Etienne, explain yourself and this nomadic person.

Etienne Ah yes, well, you see, Sophie my dear, it's ——

Esmeralda (*to Clothilde*) Wake up! Wakey! Wakey! Who are you?

Clothilde (*coming to; suddenly*) What? What?

Sophie (*to Etienne*) It's what, precisely?

Esmeralda (*to Clothilde*) What book are you from — are you

Hugo too?

Clothilde Hugo too what?

Sophie I'm waiting for an explanation, Etienne.

Etienne My dear, I can explain everything ——

Esmeralda He's very good at explaining things, he's taught me all about French Literature, haven't you Quazzi? All those meetings we've had.

Sophie Meetings — together?

Etienne Literary meetings, my dear, literature ...

Esmeralda He's such a lovely talker.

Sophie And how often were these meetings?

Esmeralda Every second Friday when his boring old wife was away. You know how it is, Marguerite.

Esmeralda nudges Sophie, who coughs

Oops, sorry. Don't overdo it, dear.

Sophie Oh, Etienne, how could you? Oh, Clothilde, how could he? (*She bursts into tears*)

Clothilde comforts Sophie

Esmeralda Very good. (*She claps her hands*) I'll do a bit of gypsy dancing later on — you're not the only good actress round here — then Quazzi can do the "bells" bit, eh?

Etienne Ssh! Please, no, don't go on about it. Let me explain — Sophie — Esmeralda ...

Esmeralda (*seeing the Porter*) Hello! And who's this then? That's three of us, Quazzi. Who's a greedy little bookworm, then? What you from, eh? Are you Molière? No. Can't be, far too modern. Are you the Madwoman of Chaillot? (*She lifts the veil*) Aargh! It's my husband!

Porter Madeleine!

Esmeralda Claude!

Porter ⎫
                  ⎬ (*together*) What are you doing here?
Esmeralda ⎭

Porter You told me that you went to confession every second Friday.

Esmeralda You told me you were a private detective.

Porter I am a private detective. I'm employed by this gentleman to follow his wife.

Sophie What? What did you say?

Porter Your husband employs me, madame, to follow you on your weekend escapades and report back to him.

Clothilde I knew I'd seen him somewhere before.

Sophie How dare you, Etienne? How dare you?

Esmeralda What a despicable thing to do. What a way to earn a living — you voyeur!

Porter You — you — strumpet!

Etienne And what did you discover? And why are you in my house alone with my wife?

Sophie, Esmeralda, Etienne and the Porter continue arguing on these themes, ad-libbing

Etienne (*finally*) Stop! Quiet! Quiet! All of you; all of us! Quiet! Let's have some order here. I am master of the house after all!

Sophie Don't order me any more, Etienne Fontaineau, after all your philandering with this creature.

Porter (*taking a notebook from his waistcoat pocket and reading from it*) "Followed Madame F. to Beauvais. Claimed to be visiting relative, instead she met Monsieur"——

Sophie Quiet, you fool! Quiet!

Etienne So! And what about *your* philandering, my dear?

Sophie Once — one time — a little spice in my life.

Porter Friday the Second of June, Friday the Sixteenth of June, Friday the Thirtieth of June, Friday the Fourteenth of July, Fri ——

Etienne Even Bastille Day? Is nothing sacred?

Sophie (*indicating Esmeralda*) And what about her? She was a
   quid pro quo.
Esmeralda How dare you! What an awful thing to call me!

The doorbell rings

Clothilde Shall I answer the door?
Porter I thought I could trust you, Madeleine.
Esmeralda At least I don't spy on people.
Clothilde I'll go, shall I?
Sophie You deceiver.
Etienne I plead self-defence.
Clothilde Someone ought to go.

Clothilde exits to the street

The following conversations are simultaneous

Esmeralda A peeping Tom.
Porter I have to earn a liv-
   ing.
Esmeralda No wonder you
   were never at home.
Porter That didn't worry you —
   until now.
Esmeralda I was lonely—
Porter Lonely — ha! Not for
   long, I'll bet.
Esmeralda You drove me to
   it.
Porter You drove *me* to it.
Esmeralda You started before
   I did.

Sophie You should plead in-
   sanity.
Etienne I leave that to your
   family.
Sophie At least we don't con-
   sort with common gypsies.
Etienne It's a costume, a costume, that's all. She's different
   when she's not wearing it.
Sophie And *you* should know.
Etienne What about your monsieur in Beauvais?
Sophie You drove me to it!
Etienne You started before I
   did.

Clothilde enters, stepping over the cases. She carries a card

Clothilde Thirty-four, thirty-five, thirty-six ... (*She coughs for attention*) Monsieur Renoir.
Etienne Show him in.
Clothilde No, he's wanted downstairs.
Sophie Who?
Clothilde Monsieur Renoir.
Esmeralda There's no-one by that name here!
Clothilde I'll tell them. (*She makes to leave*)
Porter No, wait! I am Monsieur Renoir!
Sophie You told me your name was Fragonard.
Esmeralda You told me you were Claude Monet.
Etienne You told me you were Great Aunt Marie-Louise.
Porter I — er — actually — er — am — Monsieur Renoir.
Clothilde Oh, good, 'cause your wife and four children are waiting for you downstairs.
Esmeralda What!

After a pause, the Porter dashes off through the street door, followed by Esmeralda, who shouts as she goes

Esmeralda Come here! You bigamist! You voyeur! You liar! Wait till I get my hands on you! Come here this minute, Monsieur Monet, Fragonard, Renoir or whatever you are ...

Etienne and Sophie laugh at the situation

Sophie He never struck me as artistic at all you know.
Etienne I'll bet she'll strike him — artistic or no!

More laughter

Sophie Oh, Etienne, can you ever forgive me?

Etienne Of course, my dear — if you can forgive me.
Sophie How could I possibly refuse?
Etienne Or I?

They kiss

Etienne lifts Sophie and is about to carry her off to his bedroom

Clothilde Oh, monsieur, madame, one moment — there was something else at the door.
Sophie ⎱ (*together*) Well?
Etienne ⎰
Clothilde (*presenting the card*) It's just a card that says "Looking forward to our next time together: all my love, your little — spaniel."
Etienne (*dropping Sophie*) You vixen, you're at it already.
Sophie How dare you suggest any such thing, it's you up to your old tricks. I shall pack at once and go to my great aunt's.

Sophie exits to her bedroom

(*Off*) And don't follow me, I shall lock my door meantime.
Etienne Oh, no, not that old story again. Sophie! I demand an explanation, at once. (*He starts to follow her off, then stops*) Clothilde, tell your mistress I shall be in my room when she wishes to explain.

Etienne exits to his bedroom

Clothilde Yes, sir. Oh, just a moment, I've got it wrong. This card isn't for this apartment at all, it's for the apartment downstairs. Silly me. (*She makes to follow Sophie and Etienne, but sits and looks around her*) I'll tell them in the morning! (*She falls asleep*)

CURTAIN

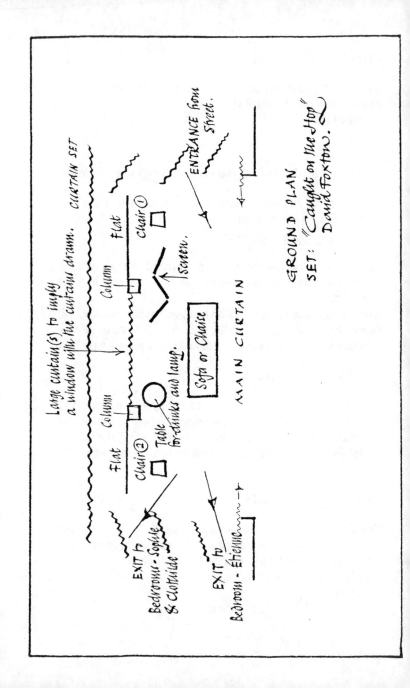

Large curtain(s) to imply
a window with the curtains drawn.   CURTAIN SET

Flat   Column   Column   Flat

Chair ②

Table
for drinks and lamp.

Sofa or Chaise

Screen.

Chair ①

MAIN CURTAIN

ENTRANCE from
Street.

EXIT to
Bedrooms - Sophie
& Clothilde

EXIT to
Bedroom - Etienne

GROUND PLAN

SET: "Caught on the Hop"
David Foxton.

FURNITURE AND PROPERTY LIST

On stage: Screen
                  Table *On it*: bottle of brandy, glasses
                  Two chairs (Optional)
                  Sofa (Optional)
                  Columns (Optional)

Off stage: Light (**Clothilde**)
                  Luggage (**Porter**)
                  Card (**Clothilde**)

Personal: **Sophie**: key (in coat pocket)
                  Porter: watch, notebook, handkerchief

LIGHTING PLOT

To open: Darkness

Cue 1:   As **Clothilde** enters   (Page 1)
Bring up a dim light to augment practical
light; gradually increase during action

EFFECTS PLOT